I0763196

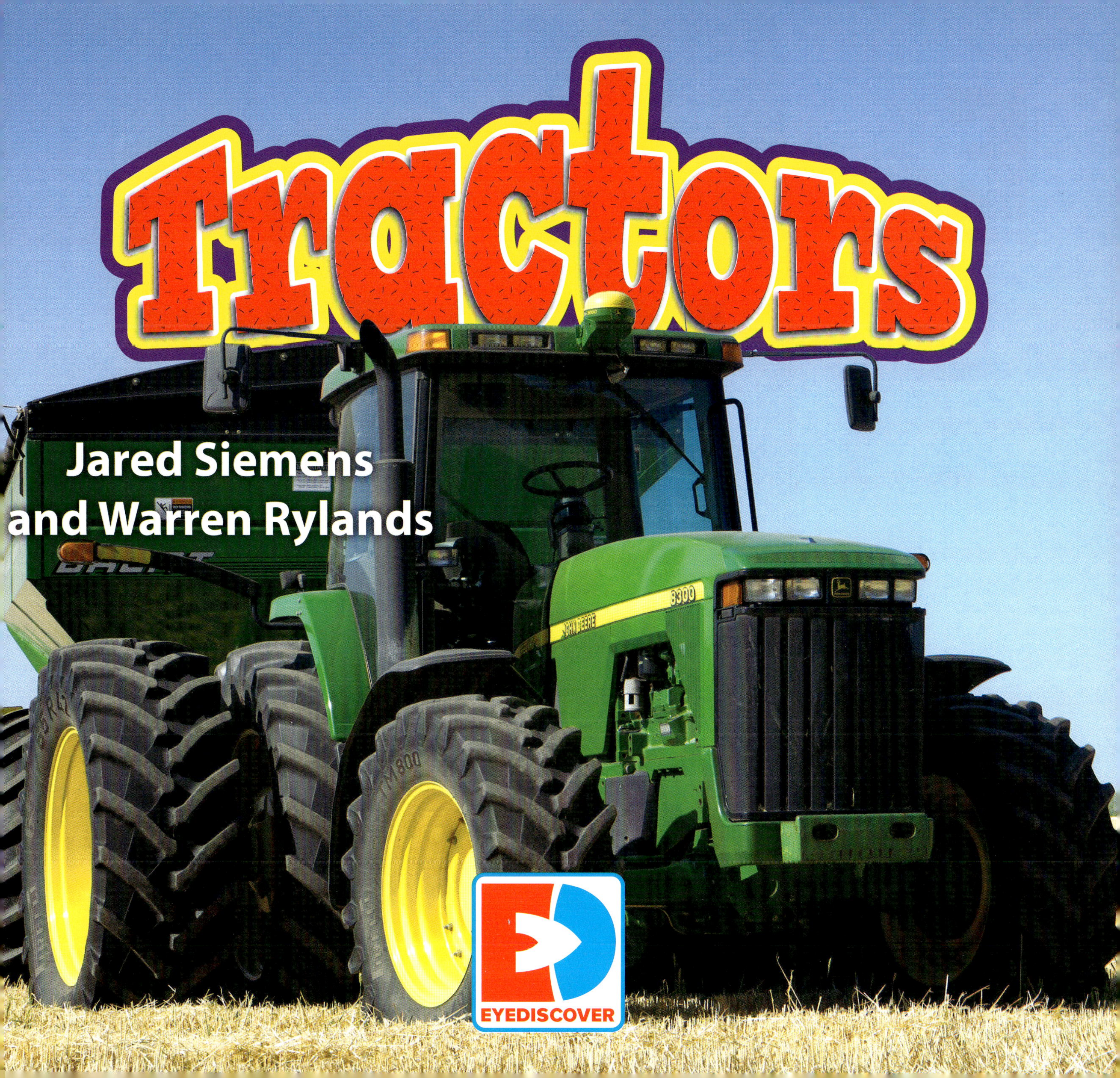
Tractors
Jared Siemens
and Warren Rylands
EYEDISCOVER

Go to **www.eyediscover.com** and enter this book's unique code.

BOOK CODE

AVT44946

EYEDISCOVER brings you optic readalongs that support active learning.

Published by AV[2] by Weigl
350 5th Avenue, 59th Floor New York, NY 10118
Website: www.eyediscover.com

Library of Congress Control Number: 2018954178

ISBN 978-1-4896-8337-3 (hardcover)

Printed in Brainerd, Minnesota, United States
1 2 3 4 5 6 7 8 9 0 22 21 20 19 18

082018
120917

Project Coordinator: John Willis
Designer: Mandy Christiansen

Weigl acknowledges Alamy and iStock as the primary image suppliers for this title.

EYEDISCOVER provides enriched content, optimized for tablet use, that supplements and complements this book. EYEDISCOVER books strive to create inspired learning and engage young minds in a total learning experience.

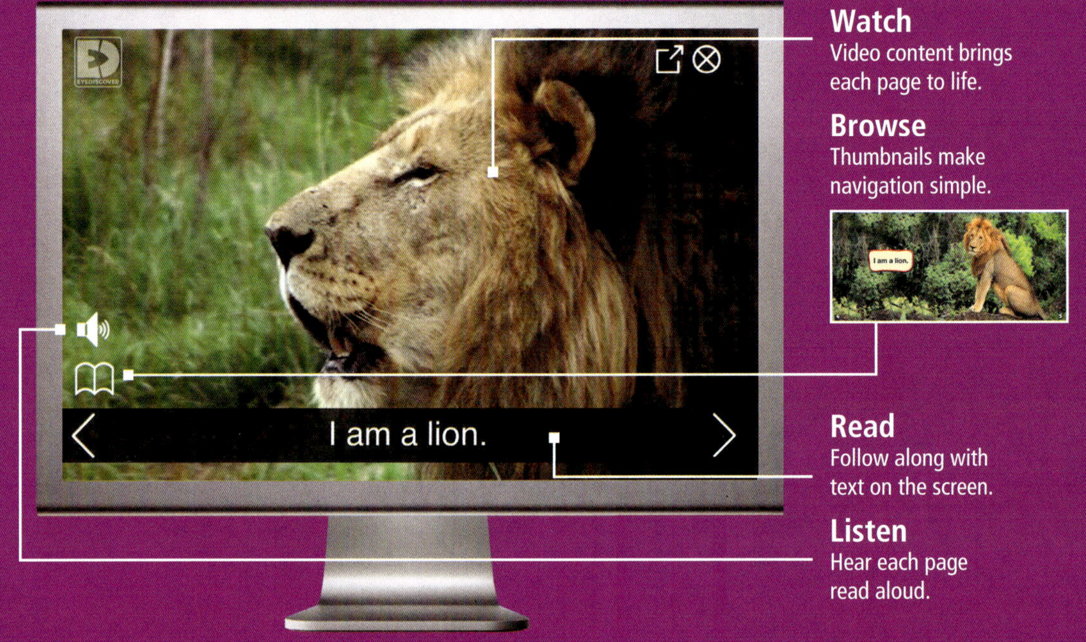

Watch
Video content brings each page to life.

Browse
Thumbnails make navigation simple.

Read
Follow along with text on the screen.

Listen
Hear each page read aloud.

Your EYEDISCOVER Optic Readalongs come alive with...

Audio
Listen to the entire book read aloud.

Video
High resolution videos turn each spread into an optic readalong.

OPTIMIZED FOR

- ✔ TABLETS
- ✔ WHITEBOARDS
- ✔ COMPUTERS
- ✔ AND MUCH MORE!

In this book, you will learn about

- what they do
- how they look
- where they work

and much more!

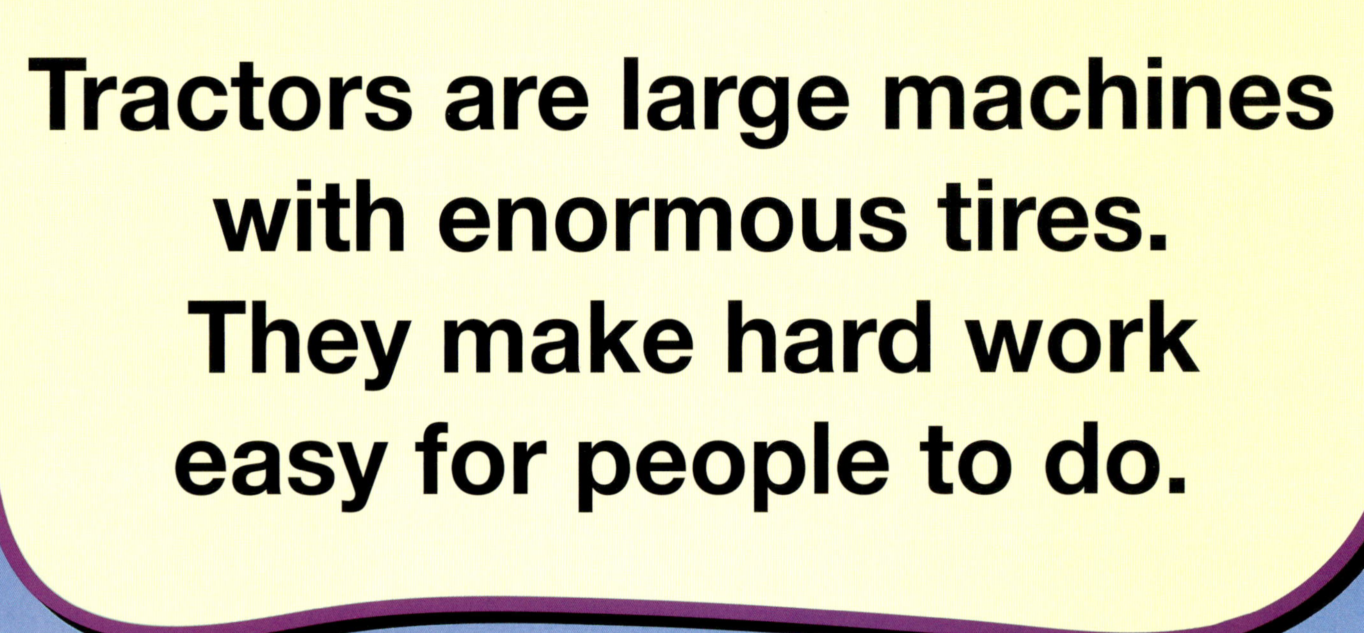

Tractors are large machines with enormous tires. They make hard work easy for people to do.

6

A tractor is slow but very powerful. It can move very heavy things.

All tractors have a cab where the driver sits. Most cabs have only one seat.

Most tractors have larger wheels in the back and smaller wheels in the front.

Tractors are used mostly on farms. They help farmers get work done more quickly.

People used horses to plow fields before tractors were made.

Farmers can add special tools to their tractors. Some tools break up the soil to plant seeds. Other tools cut hay and make it into bales.

CAT

Some tractors work on construction sites. These tractors are called backhoe loaders.

Tractors have many dangerous parts. People need to be careful when they are near tractors.

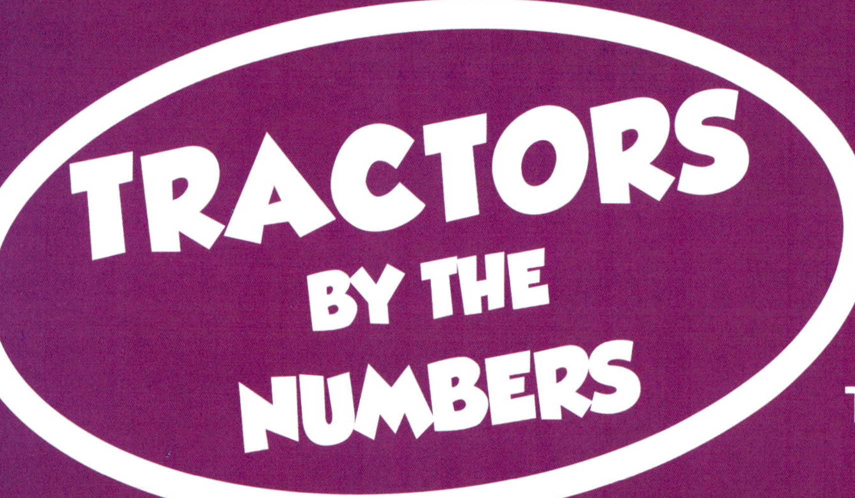

TRACTORS BY THE NUMBERS

The **largest** tractor on Earth is **14 feet** (4.27 meters) **tall**. It weighs **more than** an adult **humpback whale.**

Some **tractor motors** have as **much power** as 500 horses.

There are **more than 16 million** tractors around the world.

Some tractors can have **tires** that are **taller** than an **adult human.**

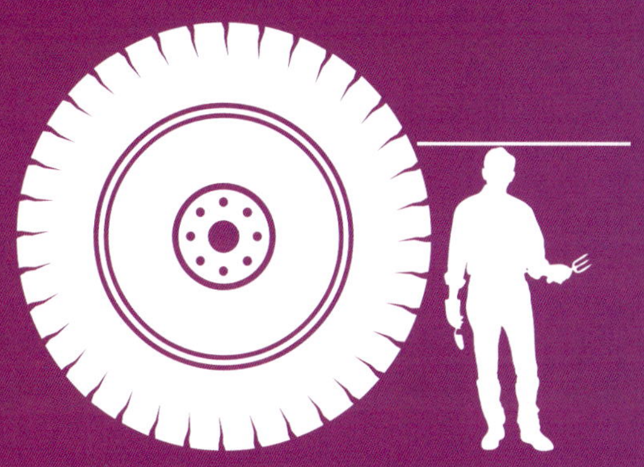

Farm **tractors** of the **future** will **not** need drivers. **Cameras** and **computers** will guide them.

John Froelich made the **first** **gasoline-powered** tractor in 1892.

KEY WORDS

Research has shown that as much as 65 percent of all written material published in English is made up of 300 words. These 300 words cannot be taught using pictures or learned by sounding them out. They must be recognized by sight. This book contains 52 common sight words to help young readers improve their reading fluency and comprehension. This book also teaches young readers several important content words, such as proper nouns. These words are paired with pictures to aid in learning and improve understanding.

Page	Sight Words First Appearance
4	are, do, for, hard, large, make, people, they, to, with, work
7	a, but, can, is, it, move, things, very
8	all, have, most, one, only, the, where
11	and, back, in
12	farms, get, help, more, on
15	before, made, were
16	add, cut, into, other, plant, some, their, up
19	these
20	be, many, near, need, parts, when

Page	Content Words First Appearance
4	machines, tires, tractors
8	cab, driver, seat
11	front, wheels
12	farmers
15	fields, horses
16	bales, hay, seeds, soil, tools
19	backhoe loaders, construction sites

Watch
Video content brings each page to life.

Browse
Thumbnails make navigation simple.

Read
Follow along with text on the screen.

Listen
Hear each page read aloud.

Go to www.eyediscover.com and enter this book's unique code.

BOOK CODE

AVT44946